For its size, a sea otter's lungs are twice as large as those of other mammals. Large lungs give sea otters more oxygen for diving—and even help them to float better.

When sea otters are in a hurry, they swim underwater on their stomachs.

1

They pump their bodies up and down, pushing hard with their hind feet to move themselves forward **1.**

A sea otter is well-suited to life in the ocean. Its flexible, cylindrical body moves through the water with ease, but drags clumsily on the ground when it comes ashore. This is because its short legs, so powerful in the water, can't support the sea otter's long body on land. Males reach a body length of about four feet and have a foot-long tail. They can weigh as much as 90 pounds or more. Females are somewhat smaller.

Sea otters are powerful and graceful swimmers, using the large muscles in their hindquarters to help them move forward in the water. The strong muscles in their forearms help them to pound open shellfish and pry abalone and mussels off rocks.

Sea otters can hear quite well, and they hold their small ears upright at the surface to listen for danger. But when diving, they point their ears downward to keep out the seawater.

The smaller and sleeker river otters have longer legs than sea otters. This makes them as agile on land as they are in the water. The many species of river otters scamper over rocks and riverbanks in North, Central, and South America, Europe, Africa, and Asia. Although one species frequents the coastal islands of Chile and Peru, none but the sea otter is adapted for a life spent at sea.

When swimming in dark or murky water, sea otters use their sensitive whiskers to feel their way around and to find food. Their whiskers also help sea otters feel vibrations in the water.

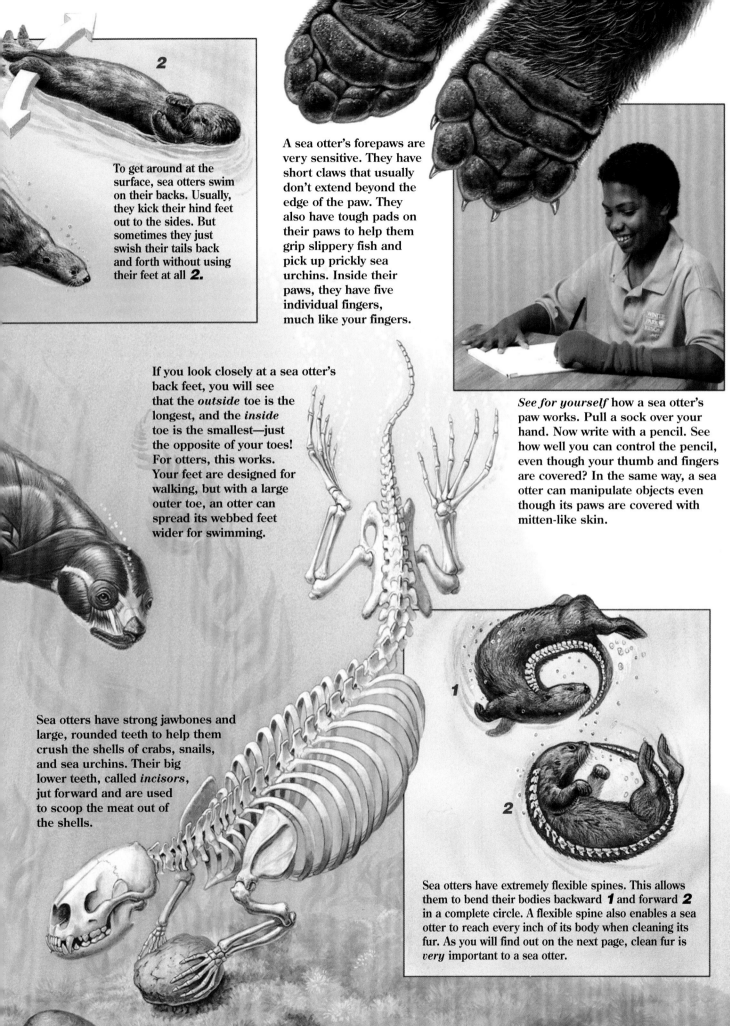

2

To get around at the surface, sea otters swim on their backs. Usually, they kick their hind feet out to the sides. But sometimes they just swish their tails back and forth without using their feet at all **2.**

A sea otter's forepaws are very sensitive. They have short claws that usually don't extend beyond the edge of the paw. They also have tough pads on their paws to help them grip slippery fish and pick up prickly sea urchins. Inside their paws, they have five individual fingers, much like your fingers.

If you look closely at a sea otter's back feet, you will see that the *outside* toe is the longest, and the *inside* toe is the smallest—just the opposite of your toes! For otters, this works. Your feet are designed for walking, but with a large outer toe, an otter can spread its webbed feet wider for swimming.

See for yourself how a sea otter's paw works. Pull a sock over your hand. Now write with a pencil. See how well you can control the pencil, even though your thumb and fingers are covered? In the same way, a sea otter can manipulate objects even though its paws are covered with mitten-like skin.

Sea otters have strong jawbones and large, rounded teeth to help them crush the shells of crabs, snails, and sea urchins. Their big lower teeth, called *incisors*, jut forward and are used to scoop the meat out of the shells.

1

2

Sea otters have extremely flexible spines. This allows them to bend their bodies backward **1** and forward **2** in a complete circle. A flexible spine also enables a sea otter to reach every inch of its body when cleaning its fur. As you will find out on the next page, clean fur is *very* important to a sea otter.

A sea otter's coat must be groomed and cleaned constantly. Clean fur is a matter of life and death to a sea otter. This is the only marine mammal without a layer of fat, or blubber, to keep it warm in the cold ocean. Instead, the sea otter's thick fur coat must keep it warm.

Sea otters have the thickest fur of any animal in the world. In fact, some otters have as many as a billion hairs on their bodies. But it's not the fur alone that keeps otters warm—a sodden, soggy coat would be cold! Instead, a protective pocket of air at the base of the fur insulates sea otters from the ocean's chill.

Because their fur is so dense, sea otters must spend a great deal of time each day grooming themselves. If they don't groom, their fur gets matted and cannot hold air bubbles. Then the water seeps through to their skin, and the cold kills them. By keeping clean, sea otters stay healthy and warm.

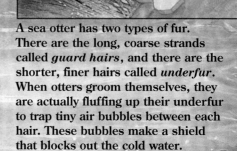

A sea otter has two types of fur. There are the long, coarse strands called *guard hairs*, and there are the shorter, finer hairs called *underfur*. When otters groom themselves, they are actually fluffing up their underfur to trap tiny air bubbles between each hair. These bubbles make a shield that blocks out the cold water.

1

See for yourself how air bubbles help a sea otter float. Fill a sink with water. Then push a dry sponge under the water. See all the bubbles coming out of the sponge as it fills with water. Now it barely floats. If a sea otter doesn't often fluff up its fur to trap bubbles, then it can't float as well either.

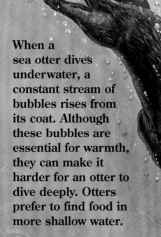

When a sea otter dives underwater, a constant stream of bubbles rises from its coat. Although these bubbles are essential for warmth, they can make it harder for an otter to dive deeply. Otters prefer to find food in more shallow water.

2

Now squeeze out the wet sponge and set it on the water's surface. Notice how it floats higher in the water. That's because you've replaced the water with air bubbles. That's just what a sea otter does when it grooms itself. It squeezes out the water to make room for the air bubbles.

4

A sea otter uses its forepaws as clamps to press water out of its fur. In addition to rubbing hard to get air next to its skin, an otter may blow into its thick coat. This traps even more air in the underfur.

Although a sea otter looks soft and cuddly, it would probably snap at anyone trying to pet its fur. Sea otters usually don't enjoy having their coats touched because this could soil their fur and be harmful to their health.

Many dogs, like this German shepherd, also have thick fur—but it's not nearly as thick as sea otter fur. Otters have at least four times as much fur on their bodies as German shepherds do.

DOG FUR

Using its sharp claws as a comb, a sea otter will scratch and brush its fur to untangle and clean it. A grooming sea otter will roll, twist, and squirm to reach every inch of its fur. Its coat is so loose on its body, an otter can pull it around to clean areas that are hard to reach.

A German shepherd has only about 40,000 hairs per square inch, whereas a sea otter can have up to a *million hairs* per square inch! If you tried to part a dog's fur with a comb, you would be able to see the skin at the base of the fur.

SEA OTTER FUR

Sea otter fur is so thick and dense it would be impossible to part it with a comb and see the skin. Because sea otters need warm coats the year around, they don't shed hair all at once like some other animals. Instead, they lose a few old hairs at a time—and grow a few new ones—all year long.

5

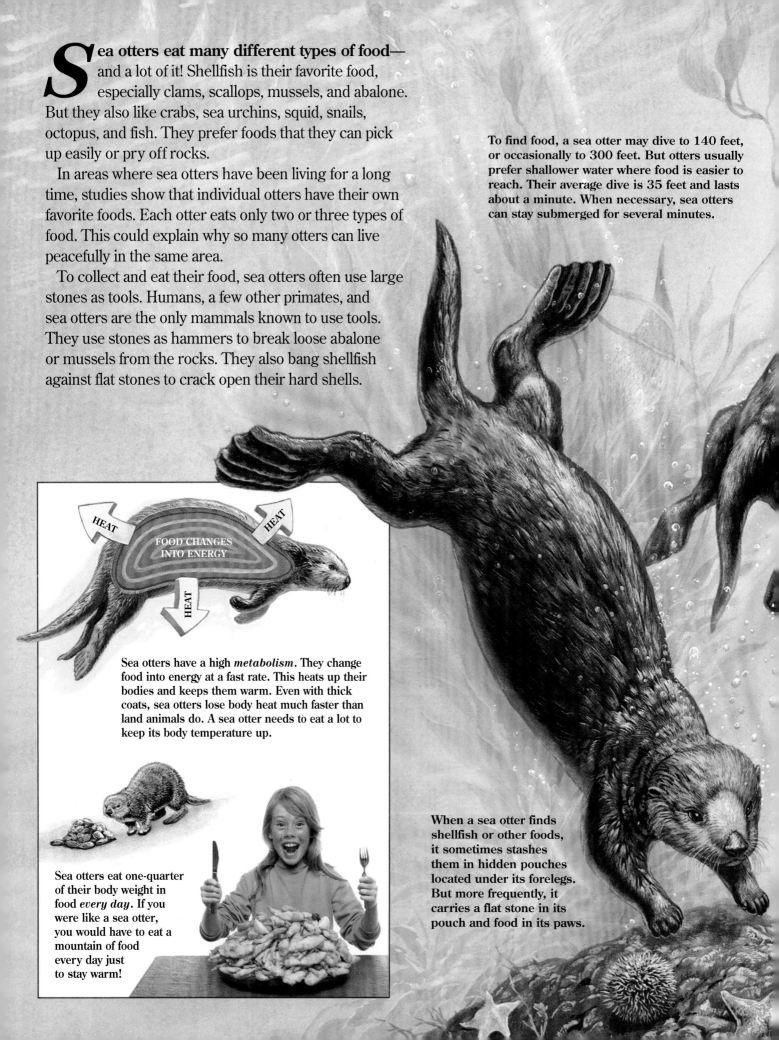

Sea otters eat many different types of food—and a lot of it! Shellfish is their favorite food, especially clams, scallops, mussels, and abalone. But they also like crabs, sea urchins, squid, snails, octopus, and fish. They prefer foods that they can pick up easily or pry off rocks.

In areas where sea otters have been living for a long time, studies show that individual otters have their own favorite foods. Each otter eats only two or three types of food. This could explain why so many otters can live peacefully in the same area.

To collect and eat their food, sea otters often use large stones as tools. Humans, a few other primates, and sea otters are the only mammals known to use tools. They use stones as hammers to break loose abalone or mussels from the rocks. They also bang shellfish against flat stones to crack open their hard shells.

To find food, a sea otter may dive to 140 feet, or occasionally to 300 feet. But otters usually prefer shallower water where food is easier to reach. Their average dive is 35 feet and lasts about a minute. When necessary, sea otters can stay submerged for several minutes.

HEAT HEAT

FOOD CHANGES INTO ENERGY

HEAT

Sea otters have a high *metabolism*. They change food into energy at a fast rate. This heats up their bodies and keeps them warm. Even with thick coats, sea otters lose body heat much faster than land animals do. A sea otter needs to eat a lot to keep its body temperature up.

Sea otters eat one-quarter of their body weight in food *every day*. If you were like a sea otter, you would have to eat a mountain of food every day just to stay warm!

When a sea otter finds shellfish or other foods, it sometimes stashes them in hidden pouches located under its forelegs. But more frequently, it carries a flat stone in its pouch and food in its paws.

While they are eating, and after they have finished a meal, sea otters roll in the water to wash off bits of shell, food scraps, and fish slime. By frequently rolling in the water, the otters keep the food from getting stuck in their fur.

A sea otter feeds at the surface, floating on its back. It takes the flat stone it has carried in its pouch and places it on its chest. Then, holding the food between both paws, it pounds the shell on the stone until it cracks open. The otter in the photo is eating a sea urchin.

People who harvest shellfish for a living blame sea otters for eating too many clams and abalone. It's true that otters do eat a lot of shellfish. But studies show that there are fewer shellfish all along the California coast—even in places where there are no sea otters! This suggests that it is *people* who are taking too many shellfish—not sea otters.

Kelp is the fastest-growing plant in the world. Kelp also provides homes for many types of sea creatures. Sea otters help kelp to grow by eating its greatest enemy—the sea urchin. Sea urchins devour kelp very quickly. With sea otters around, the sea urchin population is kept low so the kelp forest can flourish.

Kelp harvesting is a huge industry. Kelp tops are turned into a powder called alginate, which is used as a thickener in milkshakes, ice cream, and toothpaste. It is also used in frozen dinners, juices, and salad dressings as well as in vitamins and medicines. Have you had your kelp today?

Southern sea otter at Monterey Bay

ZOObooks ®

SEA OTTERS ACTIVITIES

FREE ACCESS
FOR SUBSCRIBERS ONLY

HUMPHREY'S HIDEAWAY
at zoobooks.com.,
a secret online
hangout just for kids.
Find your password on page c.

Kids Correspondence

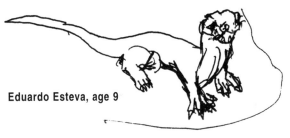

Eduardo Esteva, age 9

I saw an otter on the beach.
It was cut on one cheek.
I called Wildlife Rescue because I care.
They fixed it up right then and there.
It was on its playful way
The very next day.

Mike Lewis, age 10

I am the dancer of the water,
I am the watcher of the sea.
I will keep on swimming
'Til the love drains out of me.
A world beyond all knowings
Is where I'd like to go;
In the water I will live
And where I live, I grow.

Luke DeGregori, age 11

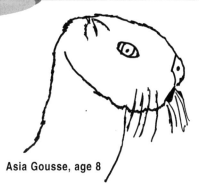

Asia Gousse, age 8

Taylor Caroline Suggs, age 11

Alexis Herrick, age 5

David Morrison, age 7

Michael Creighton, age 6

Otters swim and swim,
People walk and walk.
Otters just blow bubbles
As people talk and talk.

Annabelle Fichtner, age 7

Journie Kirdain, age 10

See More Online! Lots more stories, poems, and drawings from kids like you — *maybe even yours!* — are on our website. Lots of games, too! Your secret password is: **rafts** Turn to page **c** to find out how to get there!

Call For Entry!

Would you like to see your work published in Zoobooks? Here's what to do: By *May 1st, 2005*, we want to see your *original* poem, story, or drawing on "**Gorillas**" or "**Rhinos**." Stories must be less than 100 words; drawings must be black ink on solid white paper. Please mail them to Kids Correspondence, 12233 Thatcher Court, Poway, California 92064. Include your name, age, and address. *If your work is printed in the magazine, you will win a FREE one-year extension on your Zoobooks subscription!* Look for other entries on our website. Sorry, your work cannot be returned, and becomes the property of Wildlife Education, Ltd.

Credits: Created and Designed by Carol Prime; Additional Design and Production by Jim Webb

a

To remove, pull carefully at the arrows.

In Otter Amazement

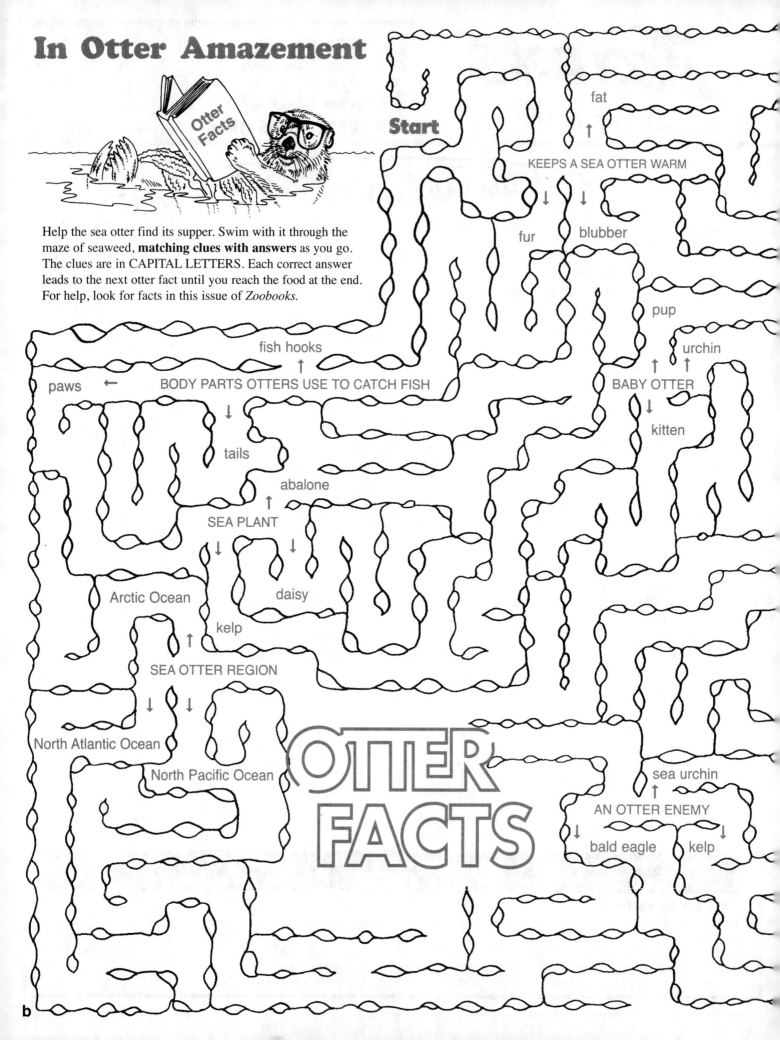

Help the sea otter find its supper. Swim with it through the maze of seaweed, **matching clues with answers** as you go. The clues are in CAPITAL LETTERS. Each correct answer leads to the next otter fact until you reach the food at the end. For help, look for facts in this issue of *Zoobooks*.

Start

fat
↑
KEEPS A SEA OTTER WARM
↓   ↓
fur   blubber

pup

urchin
↑
BABY OTTER
↓
kitten

fish hooks
↑
paws ← BODY PARTS OTTERS USE TO CATCH FISH
↓
tails

abalone
↑
SEA PLANT
↓   ↓
Arctic Ocean   daisy

kelp
↑
SEA OTTER REGION
↓   ↓
North Atlantic Ocean

North Pacific Ocean

OTTER
FACTS

sea urchin
↑
AN OTTER ENEMY
↓   ↓
bald eagle   kelp

b

Make an Otter Match

These six otters look a lot alike. But only two of them are exactly alike. Can you find the two matching otters?

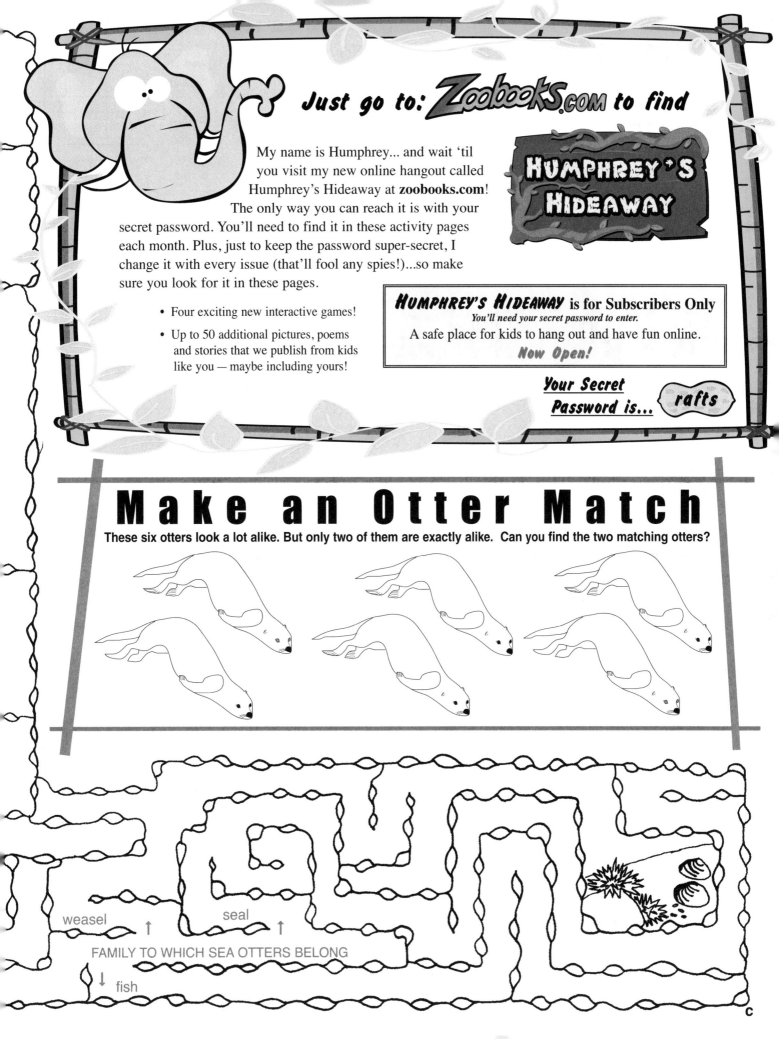

weasel ↑   seal ↑

FAMILY TO WHICH SEA OTTERS BELONG

↓ fish

What's the Point?

You can make a picture by connecting points on a coordinate graph. We made the tree on the right by marking points on a graph and drawing lines between them. We used the list of ordered pairs of numbers below beginning with **(3,2)** to make the tree.

First, we marked the point for **(3,2)**. We found the **3** across the bottom of the graph and the **2** along the side. Then, we found the point where the two numbers cross. We made an orange dot there. Then, we found the point for **(1,2)** and marked it with a black dot.

Next, we drew a black line between the two points. We continued marking and connecting points using the list of paired numbers at right (*see* Tree). Can you find all the points and connect them to complete the tree?

Now try the Main Project below. If you find and connect all 30 points, you will create a special picture. We have started the puzzle for you by marking the first two points **(0,10)** and **(3,11)** and connecting them with a black line. Use a black pen to complete the puzzle. You will be otterly pleased with the results.

Tree

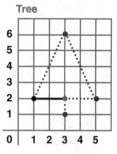

1. (3,2)
2. (1,2)
3. (3,6)
4. (5,2)
5. (3,2)
6. (3,1)

Main Project

1.	(0,10)	**7.**	(15,9)	**13.**	(18,1)
2.	(3,11)	**8.**	(16,7)	**14.**	(16,2)
3.	(6,12)	**9.**	(17,6)	**15.**	(14,3)
4.	(9,13)	**10.**	(19,4)	**16.**	(12,4)
5.	(11,13)	**11.**	(20,2)	**17.**	(11,5)
6.	(13,12)	**12.**	(20,1)	**18.**	(11,6)

19.	(9,8)	**25.**	(4,9)
20.	(8,9)	**26.**	(3,8)
21.	(7,9)	**27.**	(1,8)
22.	(6,8)	**28.**	(5,10)
23.	(4,8)	**29.**	(2,10)
24.	(6,9)	**30.**	(0,10)

Main Project

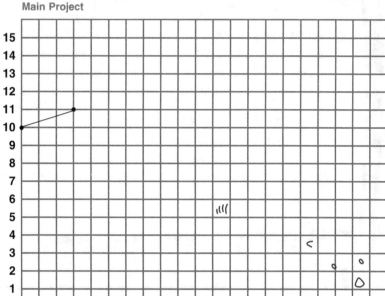

Parents and Teachers

TRY THIS ACTIVITY WITH YOUR YOUNG CHILDREN:

- Read pages 2 and 3 with your child. Allow him or her to put a pair of socks on his or her hands to see what it is like to have otter paws. Then, have your child try doing a few activities, such as eating, drawing, picking up items of various sizes, and playing catch.

- Read pages 4 and 5 with your child. Then, cut a dry sponge into the shape of an otter. Use this sponge to complete the sponge activities described on page 4. Discuss that air bubbles in the sponge help it float just like air bubbles in an otter's fur help it float and keep it warm.

- After reading the information about products made from kelp on page 7, go on a hunt with your child to find items in your own cupboards that contain alginate.

- Encourage your child to make up a story, either factual or fantastic, about the otters shown on pages 8-9 and 12-13. Tape or write down your child's story. Then, play back or read aloud the story.

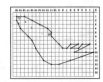

d

YOU
OTTER BE IN PICTURES

Use the pictures below to help you answer these four questions about sea otters.

1. What is a group of sea otters called? (inside front cover)

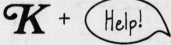

2. Why are sea otters sometimes called "old men of the sea"? (inside front cover)

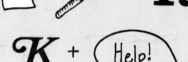

3. What grows better when sea otters eat sea urchins? (page 7)

4. What are three of the foods sea otters eat? (pages 6 and 7)

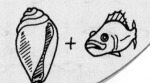

*F*ew mothers are as loving and devoted to their young as sea otters. Sea otter pups need good mothers because they are totally helpless at birth. They can barely swim. They can't feed themselves. And they don't know how to clean their fur to stay warm.

For the first month of its life, a sea otter pup rests quietly on its mother's chest as she cuddles, grooms, and feeds it. Until the pup is about six months old, its mother never leaves it except to look for food. Sea otter mothers have only one pup at a time, probably because young pups need so much attention.

Generally, sea otters are social animals. Although they feed by themselves, they often gather together in rafts to rest in their favorite kelp bed. Sea otters are the only otters that group together this way.

Sharks, killer whales, and bald eagles are the sea otter's only natural enemies. To feed its young, an eagle may swoop down and snatch a young sea otter pup from the water while its mother is off looking for food.

Sea otters spend as much time feeding at night as they do during the day—and so they nap for short periods whenever possible. Young or old, most sea otters sleep with their forepaws tucked under their chins or held over their eyes.

Sea otter pups are born on land and in the water. They weigh four to five pounds at birth. Young pups spend most of their time resting on their mothers' chests to stay warm and safe.

When a sea otter mother must leave her pup alone, she sometimes wraps it in kelp to keep it from drifting away on an ocean current. Even adult otters like to anchor themselves in kelp to sleep.

Sea otter pups love to play and wrestle with each other. Sometimes they even play with their mothers or other adult otters. Such play is not only fun, it also helps the pups develop important survival skills.

One of the very first things a sea otter pup needs to learn is how to groom its fur. And a good way for a pup to learn is by watching its mother. Pups must also learn what foods to eat, how to dive, and how to use a stone for cracking open hard-shelled food.

When escaping from danger, a sea otter mother tucks her pup under her foreleg and dives underwater. If the pup is large, she sinks her teeth into its loose fur and pulls it under. Pups are not strong enough to dive by themselves until they are two to three months old.

Mothers and pups—and other females—usually float in rafts apart from the male otters. The largest raft of sea otters ever seen was in Alaska. It had more than 2,000 members. Most rafts are much smaller, with 50 to 100 otters. In California, the average raft has only about a dozen animals.

11

A small raft of four sea otters wrapped in kelp.

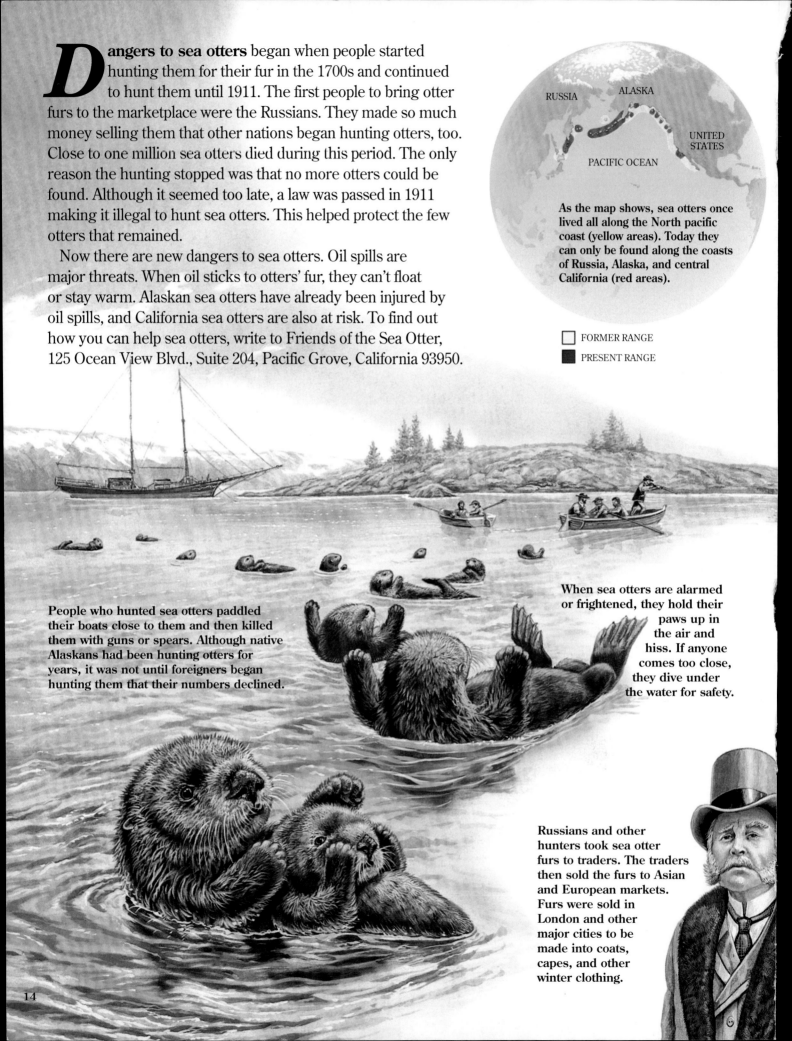

angers to sea otters began when people started hunting them for their fur in the 1700s and continued to hunt them until 1911. The first people to bring otter furs to the marketplace were the Russians. They made so much money selling them that other nations began hunting otters, too. Close to one million sea otters died during this period. The only reason the hunting stopped was that no more otters could be found. Although it seemed too late, a law was passed in 1911 making it illegal to hunt sea otters. This helped protect the few otters that remained.

Now there are new dangers to sea otters. Oil spills are major threats. When oil sticks to otters' fur, they can't float or stay warm. Alaskan sea otters have already been injured by oil spills, and California sea otters are also at risk. To find out how you can help sea otters, write to Friends of the Sea Otter, 125 Ocean View Blvd., Suite 204, Pacific Grove, California 93950.

RUSSIA   ALASKA

UNITED STATES

PACIFIC OCEAN

As the map shows, sea otters once lived all along the North pacific coast (yellow areas). Today they can only be found along the coasts of Russia, Alaska, and central California (red areas).

☐ FORMER RANGE
■ PRESENT RANGE

People who hunted sea otters paddled their boats close to them and then killed them with guns or spears. Although native Alaskans had been hunting otters for years, it was not until foreigners began hunting them that their numbers declined.

When sea otters are alarmed or frightened, they hold their paws up in the air and hiss. If anyone comes too close, they dive under the water for safety.

Russians and other hunters took sea otter furs to traders. The traders then sold the furs to Asian and European markets. Furs were sold in London and other major cities to be made into coats, capes, and other winter clothing.

14

Because sea otters sleep, raft, and feed in kelp beds, often swimming just beneath the surface, they can suffer injuries from careless boaters. Motorized jet skis are particularly dangerous for otters. Even though they have no propellers, jet skis can zip through kelp beds at top speeds—running over otters and sometimes injuring them seriously.

Fishermen drop "walls" of netting in the ocean to catch fish. They are called gill nets because fish swim into the mesh and are trapped when their gills get caught in the net. Sometimes sea otters and other marine mammals get tangled in the nets, too. Now, under California law, fishermen cannot put their gill nets in water less than 180 feet below the surface of the water. Sea otters seldom dive that deep, so the law gives them better protection.

Oil prevents air bubbles from staying in an otter's fur. If rescued quickly, an oiled sea otter can be scrubbed with dish soap to clean its coat. But even if it is rescued, it can still get sick—especially if it swallowed any oil.

Off the coast of central California, a 100-mile-long sea otter refuge was established to protect otters from harm. But even outside this refuge, sea otters are protected under the Marine Mammal Protection Act. It is important to keep the laws that protect wildlife.

To increase their range and chances of survival, Alaskan sea otters have been moved to areas along the Pacific Northwest coast. Some of these relocated otters have established new colonies.

The return of the sea otter is a success story for wildlife conservation. More than 200 years ago, seal and whale hunters, explorers, and traders thought there was an unlimited supply of sea otters. The fur thought to be the most beautiful in the world was worn by Asian royalty and was prized in Europe. Sea otters were slaughtered by the thousands. One Alaskan village exported 15,000 otter skins in a single year.

At the beginning, the curious sea otters made it easy for the fur hunters. They swam up to the boats. When they became more wary, the female otters continued to swim to the boats if their infants had been taken. Young sea otters also approached the boats if their mothers had been killed and taken aboard.

The rapid decline of sea otters prompted their early protection. But when the United States purchased Alaska in 1867, the raid on sea otters began again. By 1900, the take had dropped from almost 50,000 to 127. The sea otter that had ranged from Japanese and Russian waters to Baja California seemed doomed to extinction.

A 1911 treaty between four nations granted the sea otter protection from hunting, and sea otters eventually made a comeback. Now, the California sea otter seems to face new dangers. For the last ten years, three or four dead otters have washed ashore weekly. But in one month in 2003, 50 dead otters were found. Females tend to stay around Monterey and when sick or dying otters are found on shore, they are usually emaciated females. At present, no one knows for sure what has caused this decline in the female population. The small population increases are among the males. Males range farther south (almost to Santa Barbara), and they may find more food. Biologists suggest that there may be an environmental change in the sea otter's habitat. Diseases that most frequently attack otters are linked to sewage in the ocean. One of these, *toxoplasmosis*, comes from cat waste, which has probably been flushed down countless household toilets. Sea otters are also plagued by parasitic infections and contaminated with toxic chemicals. None of these is beneficial to otters, but so far scientists can't point to the most serious culprit.

Like all animals, sea otters have a role in maintaining balance in the natural world. The kelp that harbors other sea creatures is protected by sea otters, which subsist largely on sea urchins— the destroyers of kelp. Animals native to an environment are beneficial to their habitat. Sea otters help to maintain a natural balance along much of the Pacific coast.

A sea otter enjoys a tasty meal of crab.